ITALIAN THE EASY WAY

by

MARCEL DANESI
University of Toronto

BARRON'S

New York • London • Toronto • Sydney

© Copyright 1987 by Barron's Educational Series, Inc.

All rights reserved.
No part of this book may be reproduced
in any form, by photostat, microfilm, xerography,
or any other means, or incorporated into any
information retrieval system, electronic or
mechanical, without the written permission
of the copyright owner.

All inquiries should be addressed to:
Barron's Educational Series, Inc.
250 Wireless Boulevard
Hauppauge, New York 11788

Library of Congress Catalog Card No. 87-24195
International Standard Book No. 0-8120-3830-4

Library of Congress Cataloging-in-Publication Data

Danesi, Marcel, 1946-
   Italian the easy way.

   1. Italian language—Conversation and phrase books—
English.   2. Italian language—Self-instruction.
I. Title.
PC1121.D35 1987   458.3′421   87-24195
ISBN 0-8120-3830-4

PRINTED IN THE UNITED STATES OF AMERICA

789 100 10 9 8 7 6 5 4 3 2 1

Contents